e516

Marrewa, Jennifer
    Making a model with
solid figures.

MATH IN OUR WORLD

MAKING A MODEL WITH
SOLID FIGURES

By Jennifer Marrewa

Reading consultant: Susan Nations, M.Ed.,
author/literacy coach/consultant in literacy development
Math consultant: Rhea Stewart, M.A., mathematics content specialist

WEEKLY READER®
PUBLISHING

Please visit our web site at www.garethstevens.com
For a free color catalog describing our list of high-quality books,
call 1-800-542-2595 (USA) or 1-800-387-3178 (Canada). Our fax: 1-877-542-2596

Library of Congress Cataloging-in-Publication Data

Marrewa, Jennifer.
    Making a model with solid figures / Jennifer Marrewa.
       p. cm. — (Math in our world. Level 2)
    ISBN-13: 978-0-8368-9005-1 (lib. bdg.)
    ISBN-10: 0-8368-9005-1 (lib. bdg.)
    ISBN-13: 978-0-8368-9014-3 (softcover)
    ISBN-10: 0-8368-9014-0 (softcover)
    1. Geometry, Solid—Juvenile literature. 2. Models and modelmaking—
Juvenile literature. I. Title.
QA491.M35   2008
516'.15—dc22   2007033380

This edition first published in 2008 by
Weekly Reader® Books
An Imprint of Gareth Stevens Publishing
1 Reader's Digest Road
Pleasantville, NY 10570-7000 USA

Senior Editor: Brian Fitzgerald
Creative Director: Lisa Donovan
Graphic Designer: Alexandria Davis

Photo credits: p. 13 © Park Street/PhotoEdit; all other photographs by Gregg Andersen

Printed in the United States

1 2 3 4 5 6 7 8 9 10 09 08 07

TABLE OF CONTENTS

Words that appear in the glossary are printed in
boldface type the first time they occur in the text.

Chapter 1:
A New Park

There is a new park in the neighborhood.
The children will play at the park today.
They will have fun.

Jenny and Luis climb on the tunnel slide.
Then they slide down. Andrew and Jasmine
play on the climbing bars.

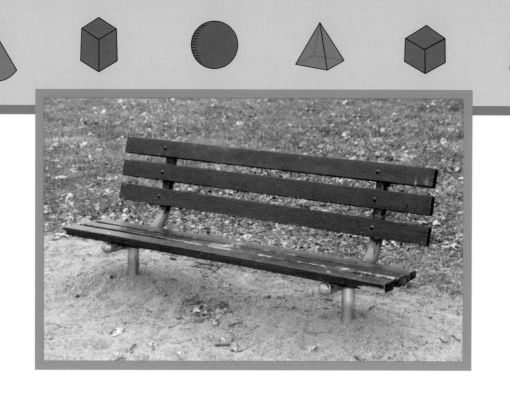

Sam and Maddie play ball. The children
sit on the park bench after they play. It is
time to rest.

It starts to rain. The children cannot play at the park now. The children must play indoors. What will they do on a rainy day?

Chapter 2:
Planning the Minipark

Jasmine has an idea. They can build a minipark. They can make a small park that looks like the real park! The minipark will fit on a table.

Everyone will collect things for the minipark from home. Then they will meet at Andrew's home. They will build the minipark there.

Chapter 3:
Searching

Jenny finds some empty paper rolls at home. They look like the tunnel slides. Jenny and Luis had fun on the tunnel slides at the park.

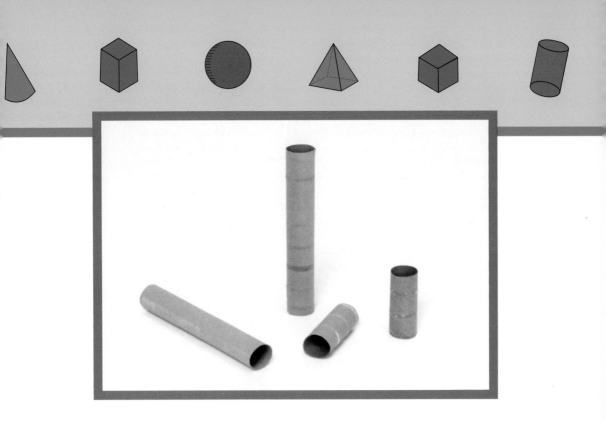

The paper rolls are **cylinders.** The tunnel slides are cylinders, too.

Jenny will bring the paper rolls to Andrew's home. She will build a tunnel slide for the minipark.

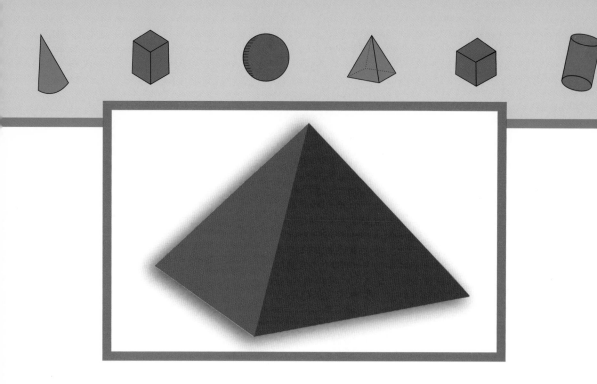

Luis looks in his toy box. He finds a
building block. It looks like the top of the
play house at the park.

The building block is a **pyramid.** The play house has a pyramid, too. Luis will bring the building block to Andrew's home.

Maddie finds a table tennis ball in the garage. She played with a red ball at the park. The table tennis ball is a **sphere.** The red ball at the park is a sphere, too.

Maddie puts the table tennis ball in her pocket. She will bring it to Andrew's home. They can put it in the minipark.

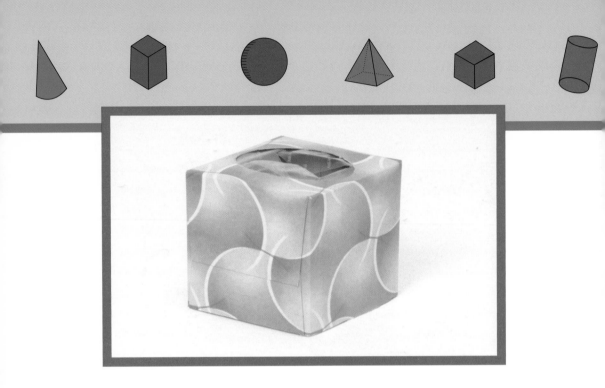

Sam remembers a building at the park.
He wants to find something that looks like
the building. He finds an empty tissue box.

The empty tissue box is a **cube.** The park building is a cube, too. Sam thinks the tissue box will be perfect for the minipark.

Jasmine saw a snack stand at the park. The snack stand had a **cone** on the roof. Jasmine wants to find something that looks like a cone.

She finds a party hat. The party hat is a cone. It looks like the roof of the snack stand. Jasmine will bring the party hat to Andrew's home.

At the park, the children sat on a bench. It was a good place to rest. The park bench is a **rectangular prism.**

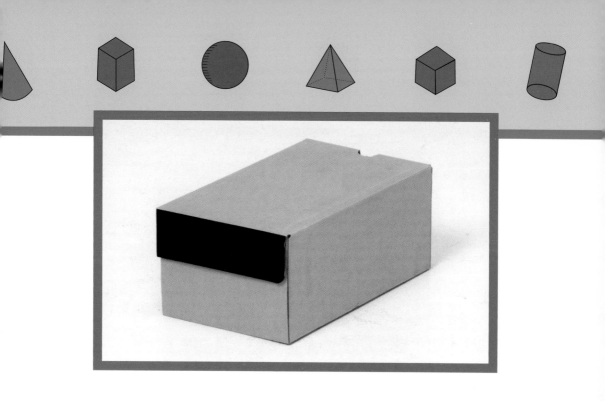

Andrew finds a shoebox. The shoebox is a rectangular prism. He will use the shoebox for the minipark. Then the minipark will have a park bench!

Chapter 4:
Time to Build!

Soon the children arrive at Andrew's home. Andrew gathers the supplies they will need. He finds crayons. He finds scissors, glue, and tape, too.

The children are excited. They share what they have found. Now they have everything they need to build the minipark.

Glossary

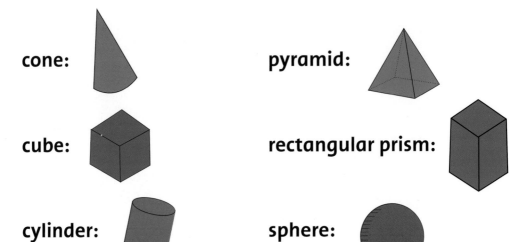

cone:

pyramid:

cube:

rectangular prism:

cylinder:

sphere:

About the Author

Jennifer Marrewa is a former elementary school teacher who writes children's books, poetry, nonfiction, and supplemental learning materials. She lives in California with her husband and two young children.